If I Do Not Reply

Tammy Lai-Ming Ho

If I Do Not Reply

Shearsman Books

Published in the United Kingdom in 2024 by
Shearsman Books Ltd
PO Box 4239
Swindon
SN3 9FN

Shearsman Books Ltd Registered Office
30–31 St. James Place, Mangotsfield, Bristol BS16 9JB
(this address not for correspondence)

www.shearsman.com

ISBN 978-1-84861-912-8

ACKNOWLEDGEMENTS

Previous versions of some of the poems appeared in *Asia Literary Review,
Berfrois, BLARB* (Blog of the *Los Angeles Review of Books*), *Cha: An Asian
Literary Journal, Cordite Poetry Review, Peacock Journal, Rhinozeros, Gallerie,
Index on Censorship: The Voice of Free Expression, Softblow, No News* (Recent
Work Press, 2020), *Standpoint, The Dissident Blog, The Tiger Moth Review,
Tupelo Quarterly, Voice & Verse Poetry Magazine*, and *WHERE ELSE: An
International Hong Kong Poetry Anthology* (Verve Poetry Press, 2023).

I would like to take this opportunity to acknowledge Ali AlShaali, Andy
Barker, Andrea Lingenfelter, Ricky de Ungria, Ricky Garni, Jarno Jakonen,
Douglas Kerr, Lucas Klein, Jason S Polley, and of course, Oliver Farry, for
their generous and helpful comments. Finally, thanks go to Tony Frazer, my
publisher, for seeing some worth in my poetry.

Contents

Part Three: Are You Becoming Critically Endangered?

Part Four: Time and Tide

For Oliver, and for Hong Kong, my eternal home.

The world forgetting, by the world forgot.

Alexander Pope

Poem with
Cantonese Sight Rhymes

Love Poem with Typos

I thought this might
museum you. You overemphasised

the poet's strangeness
and underestimated her

proclivity for embankment,
despite her being a great

pet. The sweat note
you sent her is kept in a book

whose pages are geared.
Such erudition nowadays

is no longer prised. You haven't
caused her enough bain

for her to fail
out of love, and there

won't be enough time.
You asked the poet:

Is it immortal to be teaching
such early glasses?

Sometimes a Poem

i.

A poem might argue
with itself. Its meaning is unstable,

made out of quotes. Chronically
at risk, it threatens to be undone.

ii.

A poem is all these in one: reader,
imaginary critic, eavesdropper,

denier. A poem has a subconscious
which resists understanding

too well. It gives false and incoherent
memories. A poem faces a dilemma:

iii.

to mumble everything
there is to say. To be as tight-

lipped as possible. Let the sour
chorus do the sordid work. A poem

is at its best when it feels
fierce, confident. It is as if

it lost its place for so long
and for the first time it remembers –

iv.
I am a poem. And: I am a metaphor
but not the thing. A poem is always

self-evaluating, force of habit
of a fleeting population. It hates

to be accountable for all
of it and also not much.

A poem is scared of its dissolution
through being read.

v.
A poem occupies literary spaces
its predecessors had fought for.

vi.
A poem aspires to be
subversive but only within known

boundaries, or nothing is noticed.
A poem never achieves enough.

The stakes are too low or too high,
too hard earned or unearned.

vii.
Murmurations that protect
the starlings from being preyed on

also attract the falcons, the hawks.
There, do you peer down, or up?

23 November 2022

In Some Cases Only

Being pitiful can be attractive.
Rebelliousness changes politics.
Planning for tomorrow's trip
follows weather forecast.

A person loves you back
with the intensity you desire.
No one remembers your blunders,
your uncharitable remarks.

Adding a stanza to a poem improves
it. There's understanding
between races. People who often
apologise are untrustworthy.

A coffee cup ring on a page
signifies attentive reading.
A band on the finger anywhere
means fidelity forever.

Photographs that are blurry
may end up enigmatic masterpieces.
Those who scheme are called out.
Those who work hard rewarded.

2019

Scared

My poems are scared
of shapes that stand out.
All my lines lean neatly
on the left margin.
They are scared of visual
gaps, maps, and wilful
blending of doing and being.
Scared of illusions of saying
enough or too little. Of life.
Of course, of death.

13 March 2021

Mean Poem

I write you
occasional poems for a
birthday

or a promotion,
or a journey you take,
not to attend

an imperial examination
but to show
your planning

prowess during
a pandemic.
Insignificant poems

that centuries hence
will remain unread,
untranslated,

understandably
unanthologised.
You won't live

twice,
for these poems
have neither admiring

rhymes for you
nor revolutionary
seasons.

21 March 2021

Read On

I don't know if I am pronouncing these words
correctly. They're foreign to me, and their shapes do not reveal
their secrets, unlike locomotives.
                                    But you are the poet, interjected
the disembodied moderator on the screen, sounding earnest,
However you say them must be right. Oh? That's new
to me. All right, I'll read another poem now, thank you

very much. It will make you think I'm
passive aggressive, and an exhibitionist, and focus
too much (but then not enough) the traces of my
carelessly curated history, chartless and devoid
of diagrams – the failed secretarial training (though
I type faster than you, thank you), the red wax
that burnt and covered my sister's leg

in a playground one Mid-Autumn Festival (we took her
to the hospital, and everyone else went home,
resentful), how suddenly I was a woman, and one thing
I repeated, constantly yet never heard, was Please,
don't look at me, and another, Please, please don't
look at me.

        When I finished, they asked, But, why don't
you read about your city, the one so many flee from,
the one that needs more Netflix documentaries, the one
with the upcoming…
                    Three sisters were boiling
colourful candles in two Coca Cola cans, alongside
other kids.
        One fine evening,
                                    truncated.

9 February 2021

This May Be a Love Poem

We are ugly but we have the words,
even if no one reads them.
We carry no axes, unready to kill.
Or turn on the oven until it warms.
Trains have passed us
since the day we were born
and none have crushed us.
We don't scheme to
drown in a shallow pond.
Tell me again
how you intend to dig
a grave into our bed.
And how, after all these years,
nothing else but you fills the air.
It's forever your season: loud & clear.

Found Poem: A Man Talks to Himself

David Knechtges just emailed me
to respond to a footnote.
Is beauty independent of meaning?

Abstract art is the least abstract
of the arts. It's changed a little
since the MTR station opened.

"To hang up" the phone used to be literal;
now it's metaphorical. Spoons,
maternal grandmothers, and hot pot.

Can you take poststructuralists at their word?
Modernity is the international condition
of the spelling bee.

In Mandarin, a page of a book
is an infusion. Should not it be?

Poem with Cantonese Sight Rhymes

How not to weave knowledge
into sheer hatred?
To be lenient about bad situations
with pure sentiments?
To slowly make the worst possibilities
disappear and to once again enjoy
the sun in open spaces,

hoping and pretending we're
memorialising? Are we remembered?
I'm afraid of the faint beating
of the heart of home, now loud
only in our vivid memory. Those calligraphied
banners wielded by marchers
are now objects of terror. We touch

many walls: walls of neglect
and indifference, to exchange
for rivers of when, why, and what?
Still steely, despite our frustrations
but graveyards of emotions will open
this lunar month and again.
We've created many angry ghosts

20 August 2021

Here's a Mahjong Table

I Just Don't Understand Art

A woman who doesn't know much about art was asked to comment on this painting by Winslow Homer ('Undertow', 1886). She had few words: 'I am just amazed. The detail. Everything. I don't know. I just don't understand art, if you understand me.' The art expert reassured her, 'It's about helping one another. The struggles that take place in the world that we are all part of. We work against the forces that weigh us down.' The woman looked at the painting more closely and began to tell her own story of struggle. She used words that were powerful, unpretentious, free of jargon. She used words that move me. W.H. Auden, a man of many lines, both in his poetry and countenance, once said that the masters know suffering. So many know suffering by living through it, not by poeticising, philosophising or merely contemplating. In my city which is a city of shame we see people queueing up to buy face masks – when all this is over we will be able to talk about this as though it were an absurd scenario. Some older homeless people must have woken up one day baffled as to why people were covering their faces. Would they know if they don't have a network of friends, information and bill-filled wallets? Those who have the means and power move calmly on.

Saved from the Stacks

When the libraries of my university were running out of space, handsomely bound physical copies of journals and periodicals were in danger of being transported to obscure storage locations in the city or fed to giant bins. Teaching staff were encouraged to adopt some of these publications to put them on display on their shelves in the office or at home. I remember going through the list of journals and learning later on that a colleague in my department had similarly diverse interests to mine, and we agreed, civilly, on a system of dividing up the journals undesired by others. But it was another thing about this colleague that left a strong impression in me. She lamented the students' lost opportunity to enjoy the pleasure of browsing physical books in the library and making serendipitous scholarly discoveries of their own. I remember when I was an undergraduate student at the University of Hong Kong, I would aimlessly pick out books in the library to flip through. I learnt that pages needed to be turned and the turning of the pages gave me a thrilling sensation.

Mysterious Spokes

Percival Lowell (1855–1916) was obsessed with Mars and he believed that life must have once existed there, although this was resolutely refuted by the subsequent availability of close-up photography. He also insisted that there were 'spokes' on Venus – no one else saw them, including his assistants, who took turns to sketch the planet. Later, two amateur astronomers published an article about the Venusian spokes and Lowell, revealing a fascinating fact: to see Venus, the brightest object other than the Moon in the dark, Lowell had to narrow the aperture of his large refracting telescope through which light travels. Now the telescope was more like an ophthalmoscope, used to examine the retina and other parts of the eye. Lowell had been seeing the blood vessels of his very own eye. He died believing his version of truth – the radial spindly lines on the surface of Venus. Who among us thinks we are looking afar at something wonderful only to find that we have not even left our own sight?

Ode to Age

In some cultures it is disrespectful to name the names of the deceased. In some places, people are forbidden to name the deceased. Have you finally woken up from your long sleep? In the presence of heat there may be sugar. You know it is love when your lover makes you sometimes a little surreal. You complained about the red wine, that it was inferior to me. A death at an inconvenient time is never forgotten and reminds us of the vast distance between the soil and next month. Words that sound ugly in Mandarin sound no better in Cantonese. Love that is meant to be consumed will end up boneless. We are at our happiest when we know that the happiness is hundreds of years old but is also combustible. Looking at your face, neck, and fingertips reveals no information of your permitting mind. If there were a metaphorical tomorrow I'd want to drive our desires through it like lunatics, well aware of the eyes of the watchers who jealously watch us.

Let's Not Jump into Inconclusion

One November I began to fall deeply in love with a man who just yesterday told me to add tension to my linebreaks, challenge the readers, discomfort the empty spaces on the page. I am trying to listen, but there are so many rules in the world: one must not bend the spines of books, one must not talk about sex on public transport, one must watch out for the end of the moving walkway or else one falls. Sometimes I forget his words and I ask him 'What did you say the other day that I said can be the title of my next poem?' and he has an exaggerated look of mortification because he can't recall. Without geological markers to identify directions we walk in circles. I encircle him and he me, buying each other the same books. Words are our reliable currency; so is time together. I have decided to not bother with linebreaks for three days.

Loneliness in the City

All cities by definition are lonely, their people steeped in a deep-rooted layer of sadness. Sometimes this helpless, hellish loneliness is forgotten – people are distracted by their own achievements, smiles on children's faces, satisfying food, a decent book, an evening when they see some bright stars, intense orgasms. But mostly people can't help but pity themselves and think they are members of a species beyond consolation or rescue. Their minds wander and stumble against invisible walls. Faces on the streets are persistently exhausted and ill-equipped to overcome any challenges. Faces at any given moment can flash forced polite grins. There are things that can galvanise people's genuine interest in city life but in this city, mine, the burdens of history, money, betrayal, power and choked air are too great. So few things are straightforward. So few things are truly beautiful. So much so that when I look at my loved one's wise eyes, I ask myself: Can this happiness be real, pure?

Time is the Only Important Ingredient

What are the most prophetic hours in any given day? You claim so convincingly you were born in the same year as the start of modern Chinese poetry that I urge you to write a slim book about it, which will be read by eight people, if you are lucky. I stay one step ahead of you, sometimes two or five, and you are annoyed, not because I am a woman, but because I am right. Our prefrontal cortices can transpose us from here to there, and from now to another time, a super power that allows us to imagine the gifts that we haven't bought yet and the numerous raw encounters that aren't yet ours. Our lovemaking transcends time; it is fluid, fluent, flawless: a perfect combination of body heat, textures and the duration of frisson. Time passes faster for our faces than other body parts when we are standing up. But what if people are experimenting horizontally? There are always deadlines, and they are always sooner than we thought, and some involve literal deaths. Our Earth is spinning slower than the time when the dinosaurs were alive, while our room, the number of which you don't care to know and could be 2046, doesn't spin at all. We know light takes time to reach us and everything we see is in the past. How can that be? Now my right hand is on your smug face, which I see and want to kiss and all this feels very now. Has the moment passed?

Measures

When I don't know what to say I silently count coins and he's annoyed by this act. Even if he loves me completely, let us be honest, it is still not enough, because completeness is relative. If I could upturn his books carefully numbered and lined up on the shelves – calligraphy scrolls lend the arrangement a learned aura – I would. I hear his voice and I sometimes quickly calculate: am I today totally loving, or do I allow myself to be difficult? A city is ruined only when a certain percentage of its physical appearance is no longer recognisable. A relationship is ruined despite everything looking intact; the lovers' phones tell the right hour, their laundry out to dry is clean, they go to the theatre to be seen. Many languages are tonal and they don't require more attentiveness except when what is said is said with attention. At the end of a meal, he watches me suck the remaining chopped bird's eye chillies, spitting out the spent red skin that glistens darkly. He knows my lips are all at that time hot and swollen, ready to be soon kissed on our bed, where we count our four hip bones.

Potential Last Words: A Selection

Half a pint of love. Have I been trying hard? The clouds today seem so beautiful. What is wrong with my toes? The incessant cries of the devil. You really dislike potatoes? The silent letters mustn't be omitted. Can I chase after the paper planes? My children are not learning. Are you sorry now? Everything is so far out. Is the city getting better? You are all whispering. What will you do with the heat? Don't put me in an urn. Should I have regrets? That night, the river was very still. Will you tell my mother I hid it in her closet, the old one? Rosebud. Is this real life or fantasy? Please finish my translation. Why are you staring at my face? I have to make it secretly obvious. Is it already June? I am not ready to go. Who wrote that poem about raging? I saw blood everywhere but they said it was thick dirty water. Can you remain hopeful? Put down your fucking phone. The job is not done yet? I have no enemies. Do you hear the people sing? My life is finally mine, mine. Is he still exiled? Open the blinds and look out. Am I indeed mortal? They did everything to keep us asleep. Promise me you won't lie to me again. I only have one son and he's stillborn. What are they calling China? Be not afraid. They still tell that false narrative? I am in love with another man. Are there squares within squares and circles? I have no last words.

Here's a Mahjong Table

I looked at this cover of *London Review of Books* by Peter Campbell and wondered if other readers of Chinese also see a make-believe character in black ink. A mixture of 'West' and 'Country'. How have I been conditioned to see the random overlapping or lonely lines and shapes as potential Chinese characters signifying meanings not yet entirely known? We are allowed to read literary texts as self-contained and self-referential. Some will see Campbell's work as abstract: here's a pair of earrings, here's a girl playing hopscotch, here are two mathematical signs. Here's a mahjong table. Some others, like me, who read Chinese, will persist on translating the artwork into a form they understand. Yes, I will translate you into a form I think I understand and I will misread you. Only slightly.

On the Day of the Eclipse

The sky doesn't open. Uncharged light bulbs explode into glowing fragments. There are three ways to recognise the smell of a sun-shaped onion: boiling, peeling, and crying. Some people look directly at the eclipse and imagine themselves fainting; they dream of thousands of arrows pointing towards a giant clock face, its numbers written in pre-digitised Chinese. ONE (一) is the smooth back of a wet elephant. TWO (二) is a training step for infants. Some say their names or birthdays coincide with the natural phenomenon and ask: Is the moon a sun in another macrocosm? Poets wonder if they should write poems, photographers click their shutters from a distance. A pregnant woman accidentally sees the partially covered sun will give birth to a healthy son. Can the sun really be stolen, eaten and spat out, by an ancient dragon? The seconds and minutes are being counted: all worlds collide, all instances. An invisible and unwanted timeline for this city, like mysterious corpses, washes up in the harbour, cannot be debunked. Tomorrow, once again, the sun calls on us in bed. We make it stand still for a moment, we make it run.

21 June 2020

Allegories

Picture the ocean, those who believe they are destined for it until they are missing or go mad. The gradual merging of land and water, at first subtle, then final. On neglected streets in odd cities there are still walls that have retained memories of the long third day. Imagine being a mollusc enlarging its shell to accommodate the growth of its body, carrying the burden of self-protection when pushing its way across its pitiful lifespan. Despite attempts at humanity, each island of us can be deluged under the sea wearily weeping, which lasts merely seconds or a whole century.

Far from the ocean, rocks grow metaphorical legs and move to unsuspecting rivers and streams. They break down during this audacious journey and are prepared for further parting. When they reach the ocean, they are broken and broke. The battering waves grind and mangle them like a practical joke into sand. In each grain is a history, a struggle. Examine it with curiosity, with composure.

Under the sea, at night, at dusk, howling grand geological events cause tsunami waves. They build up heights, higher and loftier, faster and in tremendous conviction, whenever they travel inland. When the land is submerged, remember I have warned you about water's seductive persistence. A recital is now going on, past midnight, across years of two animals. Do not be surprised at waves coming back, unending, unextinguished. Do not.

12 February 2021

Are You Becoming Critically Endangered?

Begins Mid-May

Writers take stories from city to city.
Some people read in the airport, about cruelty,
'unforgivable havoc'. The night heaves into day,

windows juxtapose. Only the cushions,
overnight, fall silent. Chinese calligraphy
meets full-gear missions.

It is impossible to replicate a certain kind of love –
every political movement has a unique tune.
We are each a pair of parentheses,

an outgrown womb, explicit.
Our flesh takes on additional hues. The tongues
learn new and swiftly crystallised slogans.

At some point, behind closed gates,
some are missing. No right nouns
or verbs can narrate hidden chronology.

Sentences about us begin mid-way; enough
light comes through. Enough hope.
We continue to be with this city.

Leftovers

The Chinese understand leftovers.
How food can be made over into other food.
How whatever's left in the pot can be reused,
cooked into something random, humble.

That women still unmarried
in their early thirties or beyond
are called *sheng nu* –
literally the 'left-over ladies'.

And why 61 million children
have been left over, left behind in villages
by parents seeking work in cities,
living in cramped spaces, eating leftovers.

Crude Insistent Passion

At which point we are beaten
we stand up again
against the brickbats

of unvarnished tyranny.
At which point we despair
we remember

the conception of hope
and the daily chanting
of our identity.

Every Hong Konger
who has a conscience
is my rising sun. Our fight

is organic, like the heart
that beats
into a dignified introduction.

We are humans; we bleed,
shake in anger, and love,
not yellow objects lost,

kicked about
by Asia's finest. The future
is embedded in the past,

which beckons now.
We are unafraid
of blanks,

which we will fill in
with diligent
anticipation.

*This poem was written on 29 September 2019 and it makes reference to an
incident on 21 September 2019, when a protester in a yellow shirt was beaten
by the police and later called a 'yellow object'.*

Neighbouring Sounds

What is the hour of the day
when most people are awake?
Awake to the sounds of cars honking,
being directed to other routes.
Someone smashed three glass doors,
while in the distant world
forest trees, not trash cans, are burning.
Waves carrying naked, dead bodies
to the shore. But they don't make a sound.

The hour when people
are woken up to the city anthem played
in various instruments, and nobody
is deprived of her triumphant music.
Bullets travel at speeds greater
than the speed of sound – a sonic boom reverberates.
Some muted voices ride into the night,
never to resurface as before.

There are cycles of wakefulness
around the world. The ticking of this clock
descends upon us. Hongkongers
are awake, awake, awake.

Thursday 17 October 2019

Brushstrokes

Today a language is released
somewhere. It advocates
the importance and sometimes
unjust uses of sentences.

Connections are made,
while people's health is cautioned.
There are rights that are expected
and not fortified. Surveillance

places schools in restricted
zones. Linguists define a campaign
to supplant ethnic minorities.
When access to power lines

is immediately shut down,
information commands respect
and prominent control –
alongside vicious tongues

online. Behind different types
of detentions are discrepancies
in the hues of sky, independent walls,
sounds of crackdowns

at condemned dawns. Performance
artists drop all their coins;
poets no longer led by waves
of brutal hopes. What they are now

about and their whereabouts
remain unknown. Excerpts
of thousands' lives are watered
down. Bold broad brushstrokes.

2 February 2021

Doubtless

Doubtless some people's reactions are dulled to night pictures of Hong Kong showing untypical street sights that have been reverse alchemised into regularity. Doubtless it is no longer surprising a district famous for its temple where citizens go to pray for good health, good grades, good marriages, harmonious families, and speedy promotion at work, should also be covered with teargas smoke as if by drifting clouds. Doubtless a people are propelled to be creative with words and images when so many of their protective gear is homemade, taken from thousands of homes.

Doubtless some pictures still tug at the heart. Doubtless even the most landlocked part of the city becomes part of the Be Water movement. Doubtless our attentive inventiveness is part of our strategy.

4 August 2019

To Thine Own Self Be True

A typical night when extended family congregate to feast, except this is nothing typical. It is a repeat of 2014 when yellow umbrellas bloomed across the city. Now someone says all protesters are rioters, disrupting Hong Kong's daily routine with bricks and kitchen implements. Now another says check your source of information. I bit my tongue so as not to cause an explosion. The ones who raised me see only one-sided news. Are we separated just by a TV channel? The streets that I walk past to get to my Sham Shui Po home are covered in smoke. It is surreally beautiful, like a music video, but incongruous to the humble shuttered shops. Sleepless nights beckon conscience. Do we turn a blind eye, or do we fight? A city of people reevaluating life, calculating what is worthwhile. I look at myself in the mirror: why the hell can't you do more?

7 August 2019

Simplicity is Not an Option

Even the computer keyboard
overhears the never-ending sounds

of shouting. People
teach themselves and others

how to plant traffic cones.
Goggles wear young faces –

not swimming but rising.
They walk towards me in dreams,

on a landscape
of billowing acrid smoke.

Artificial fog everywhere:
Fog in residential areas,

fog in homes for the elderly.
Lived lives confront lives lived –

We were the same, but now
speak different dialects

of gear. In schools they don't
teach the scenario

of running away
from being gassed.

9 August 2019

The Eye

A crater, a window, an entrance to the soul, a lone well, an empty dish, a lamp to the body – is collectively mourned; heartbreaking and haunting. A young woman lost an eye in her beloved city, the result of certain people already having turned half blind. One eye open, one eye closed: only surveilling, seeing selective sights, scenes and sins. Hong Kong was once lost, and then found, and lost, and will be found again; a cycle of blood, sweat, and tears.

12 August 2019

Laid Bare

Once upon a time we were ignorant
of tear gas inside MTR stations
and in fact, of tear gas.
We marched on planned routes
and the next day, returned to work,
school, and naïvely conceived normality.
Now it is no longer possible
to feign innocence: Blood
of protesters shed on the streets,
thick and clearly witnessed.
The flaws that make our society now
are the flaws of tyrants.
Fearful but defiant trapped birds,
we are in a deadlocked situation,
but still tuned to the tone
of freedom, dreaming of breathing
free, sighting streets of regular traffic,
each others' faces.

12 August 2019

Nights

i.

NIGHTMARES – All my nightmares last night were about the protests. In one the police spray not gas but tattoo ink at the protesters so they are marked and identifiable. In another, the city has descended into general chaos but a wedding is still going ahead in a darkened open space with bright threads of fires in the background, everyone wearing heavy gas masks. In yet another I am walking on an LRT platform in Yuen Long or Tuen Mun. The platform is covered in post-its; I stop and read, and to my horror they are in a language I can't understand.

ii.

HONGKONGERS – One of the most memorable experiences I have had while marching this summer is that *anyone* can shout 'Hong-kongers 香港人!' and the crowd nearby would respond 'Add Oil 加油!'. This call and response, this solidarity, this strong demonstration of love for the city, is remarkable. Leaderless – but any given moment, anyone can lead, then another person will take over. And another. And another. And another.

iii.

THINGS TO WRITE ON – Anti-communism, dismantled huts, bitter chocolate, cigarette butts in a urinal, the haunting sound of snow melting over sewage drains, oversized pigeons, quarantine, failed first kisses, yoga-loving murderers, Sebald's photographs, fish-net stockings that have just been peeled off, 'From the dusty mesa / Her looming shadow grows / Hidden in the branches / Of the poison creosote'. Orchard, orchard, orchard. No. Yes. Maybe. Tomorrow.

August 2019

One Person

If I tell you my full name, will you only say it when I drown or fall? Which protest poster will you carry around close to your chest like an oversized pendant? Have you been served gas or spray? Where to meet next, a nearby MTR station or the airport? When they used water cannon they hijacked our story – our story. Can we rehearse running away, not from our family, but from the gangsters, the police? Can you chant louder, please? We don't have a microphone or an elaborate stage. Tell them not to look at us as though we are in a clichéd narrative. Sometimes, when we are all together, I just want to see one human face. All the voices in the dark enlivens this street in the poorest neighbourhood in Hong Kong. You are in my memories, emerging from engulfing smoke, your helmet broken in symmetrical halves. Don't tell me sleep is good when armed men with dazed eyes are still out there. Throughout epochs, time is the epitaph, the answer. Remember: history will not desert us. We are everything: the pavements, the schools, the little shops, the young women violated, the protest songs sung over the Chinese national anthem, the placards that enthusiastically say Add Oil, the walls covered with post-its and graffiti: 'You taught me peaceful marches are useless'. The moon does nothing but watches, for she knows our destiny. It mourns lives lost. We are time and we witness and we flow, in motion, but we are not silent. One of us holds up a sign, millions of us mouth the same words, solitarily, across this tiny, insignificant port city, which is my city. Millions. Millions.

5 September 2019

Open Secrets

i.

My mother's eyes are dry but tears
sometimes find their way there.
The woman selling dead seafood keeps
wetting the lobsters with ice water

near the shore where tourists cheer and wave.
A paper kaleidoscope has limited
use but it is a birthday present, along
with a house and a plasticine key that is too big
and a red hand-painted card. The skin
does not heal itself fully when hurt; lifeless
flakes on the sofa, desk, everywhere black.
One copies a poem in dark sour ink,

the Chinese characters escape in rain.
An abstract ship sailing, not yet stranded,
blurry nests. It heads to the future, already,
the sky is ripening. Like a beard grown.

ii.

Please wait. We'll be with you in a moment.
The walls grow impatient; no more
breathing through the cracks of hope. How
many are still counting? Closed curtains

day and night. Rumours say if everyone
writes in shorthand or distorted
script, we might be heard, understood
as millions of distraught, distracted
masked mouths. There's a saltiness

in the books with titles that spell city, speech
and shock. Which part of the face
is the loneliest? We have come so far,
and not far enough. Stuffed animals
on delayed parades, some dressed like
frogs and ducks. Three-dimensional
time has gone on. Narratives are stuck.

iii.

I dream often of you in an unfamiliar
shirt or half-naked, your back beaten. You
are many faces but I know none
closely: and none are returning

home in an instant. Seasons
don't change when they are of grief
and tightened limbs that are paused.
They still invent new rules
drawn on harsh desks behind closed
doors and we use the same symbols
with conviction like the weathering
stones and umbrella bones.

Spotless, this year, is a fantasy.
Galloping images and sounds await
simultaneous interpreters whose headsets
are in disarray. Who is listening?

iv.

I am bad at graphs, charts,
and calligraphy that magnifies facts.
If Hockney is not an iPad artist,
I'm not a poet of protests

but someone who cautiously writes
about Hong Kong. The city's streets
are easy enough to navigate. Taxi
drivers say they can't fool
passengers. But I have seen roads
blocked and signs altered creatively
to send us messages. Love
is not only conditional, relative,
but a wilful white car in a storm.
Holes in the street, window panes
on curved buildings turned yellow
with slogans you know. We know.

v.

I sit hunched on a pavement
in Wanchai, too early for a meeting
about art, poetry, photography. They
have repeatedly drawn our attention
to neon signs that glow
but throw no shadows that footsteps
can make explicit. My fellow citizens
walk home after work, purposeful
but, in truth, directionless,
in anticipation of a sofa that lets
them linger maskless. I slalom
between moving cars and trip
over the wheels of parked ones.
Chewing gum blackened on every street
testifies to our troublesome existence.
If there's a tomorrow, it's already here.

vi.

There's a hurricane path
cutting through everyone's mind;
we're all a little insane now. An eel
trained to needle through penetrating
thoughts. People say our belts
are fastened too tight in this part
of the world; freedom is only free
when guaranteed. We frame
everything like Zoom windows;
restaurant tables partitioned
with makeshift dividers, on mathematical
principles. I'm convinced it's art,
worthy of permanent international
exhibitions. The food deliveryman asks,
'Are these coins clean?' Laundry day
comes again. Dust settles.

November 2020

Licking Graffiti on Cement Walls

i.

The dream I had before waking up this morning:
A cat jumping up to the sky
and using her mouth to grab a bird
in flight. Both of them
fall to the ground, impaled
on nails. As they die,
they are panting, breathing out
feathers.
Their fierce eyes stare
at the immensity of brick structures
on Junction Road, Kowloon Tong,
standing like ancient dolmens.

ii.

In another dream
I am buying fishballs
from a streetfood shop
in Sham Shui Po. Suddenly
teargas smoke engulfs everything,
and even the pieces of food
want to wriggle free
from their skewers.
Two youngsters
walk towards me to offer help.
In my dream, under their plain masks
are the faces of mere infants
forced into playing the role of
protesters.

iii.

In one dream
I am sitting
in an upturned 7-11 umbrella,
gliding in the sky, away
from toxic teargas smokes,
in a part of my city
that could be anywhere.
But the umbrella is pierced
by bullets and it plummets.
My blood on my inner thighs
stains the umbrella, as though
I am having a miscarriage.
My palms disappear
and I can't reach my phone,
can't raise my hand
to call for help. I think
of leaving behind a mental note
but I have no words.

iv.

I dreamt I was inside
a coffin
flowing in sewage.
I could see a flash light
that flickered &
stopped.
Then I was no longer
in the coffin but lying
naked on the ground
of the cavernous inner
courtyard of the Tuen Mun
public housing building

where I grew up.
I had become a ghost.

v.

In a dream I woke up from
after having intense pain
in my right calf,
everyone's face is covered
with dripping blood. Some
are singing or praying,
but no sounds come out from their mouths.
Some have hands
that are no longer shaped
like hands. Some have broken
collarbones on which industrial face masks grow.
Some lose their sense of smell
and lick graffiti on cement walls.
We have become a city of freaks.

Writing Despite Inarticulateness

Not because of censorship. I fear
no knock on the door before dawn,
nor the expressions of concern
from friends. But rather the sleep-deprived
nights of thinking what to do,
what can my generation do,
and the next, and the next.

The trees that were planted
will not die unless wilfully uprooted.
The songs sung by birds of freedom
continue to exist, in some form,
in this universe. But the time taken
from those wrongly imprisoned
murders something in all of us.

Can we stop and think,
and not only about shoes, sushi,
electronic cigarettes. Drinks,
artisanal or otherwise. Think:
what this city means today,
and how in less than thirty years
it may be no more. No more.

A Lie and a Promise

Missing people are missing
people too. The list,
whatever list, cannot be updated

fast enough
to meet everyone's imagination.
Some people have enough hurt

to debut newer hurt. There are exactly
two types of governments.
It must be nice to feel okay to speak

and then not speak and then speak again.
Are all your documents renewed, all in line?
Have you a nom de plume?
A lie and a promise

in Chinese is the difference
of half a character.

7 August 2021

Fetch

I've grown tired of aquatic metaphors,
especially those about my city.
The other morning I saw a dog in the sea
excited to swim far out again and again

to retrieve a toy bone thrown
by its absent-minded owner next to the shark
lines. Was it the fake chewed bone?
The freedom of movement

in water? The familiarity of the routine?
The small triumph in closing the distance
between the body and what is outside
of it? I can't interrogate what prompts

joy in dogs or fish, but I remember
that whole moment and me in it –
becoming an agentless metaphor.
To thine own happiness be too.

8 August 2021

All Told

In a face: a garden,
a valediction, a validation, a
kaleidoscope, already a

graveyard. There can be
too much face
on a face. Speak to it,

can it talk back? Literally,
figuratively, facially, philosophically. New
faces growing out of a face

centuries old and rotting, barely
concealing or cancelling
its nightmares. New faces

with fresh layers of skin, in-
congruous and hideous.
From where? Disgrace

is earned, faces
given by others. This monster
isn't Frankenstein's, but

hey, we've created it.

10 August 2021

Wait

Perhaps a potted plant can wait.
Paint on public walls soaked
by Hong Kong torrents can wait
to be covered up. The
pillowcases, now worn, once
purchased to match
the purple curtains, can wait
to be replaced, while the
blemishes in the corners
of the wedding frames can wait
to be smoothed over.
Who can afford to wait
for the pandemic to pass?
Today: sitting ducks sitting and waiting
for the city's earth to be scorched
clean of anything of sustenance.
What else can be done but wait?

12 August 2021

Sketching a City

When the government says
it's all ears, ears breed
on its face –

for a visual performance.
Small craters of flesh
and cartilage collect

polluted dew
instead of listening.
The public have lost

aspiring arms and legs
in housing. These unattached
limbs threaten to form

an empire. If certain clouds
above the city are cut open
while under the knife –

thousands of indifferent
heads emerge.
The wealthy and the fearful

wash their perfected
hands of freedom,
while scores

of stuck-out necks
are wrung
into unresolved knots.

At risk of being truncated,
some hands still write out
what the hearts dictate.

People are raging –
so angry their boiled blood
could flood

the once acclaimed,
illustrious harbour.
Take a look.

Look closer.
Those are cried-out hearts
on the far shores.

27 October 2022

Formerly

I wanted to walk by my old
apartment block to just

check if the elephant-
shaped flower pots

were still there near
the barber shop. It's fine

to choke up when you see
abandoned windows no

longer lit up in the evening
just as it is not at all shameful

to pity a worried ant trapped
in an inscribed circle

16 November 2022

Tomorrows

If I walk on a Hong Kong street
for long enough,
I will eventually bump into someone I know
from a long time ago. So long ago
that each of us wilfully resorts to
deceptive amnesia.

There are streets in this city
that are almost unwalkable:
they are too neat, they lack
cigarette smoke, the old women
no longer sit on the pavement.

Sometimes a word said by a stranger
presents itself intimately, enters my ears
like a curse. I turn around,
it's a group of shadows
counting tomorrows.

The Visitation

My paternal grandmother came to me
in a dream and said:
I have no money and I'm cold.
I recounted the visitation to my parents –

They had forgotten to burn
for my granny paper money,
paper clothes – offerings
sent to the fire and received

by imaginary ghosts.
Except I hadn't imagined granny's
animated agony. It was a song she sang
when dealing Hakka cards:

I have no money and I'm cold.
I have no money and I'm old.
For years I haven't seen these cards,
their characters now even more foreign.

I remember the strangeness
of the names the cards were called.
White strands in a water basin
when granny slowly washed her hair.

The humble dishes she cooked
in the warm windowless kitchen:
lean pork, steamed egg, rice in soy sauce.
Her lingering odour in summer.

Talking to a friend, Hakka words barked
into the receiver of a black rotary phone
with a long curly cord.
I sat there, understanding it all.

Now, I sing her song
on an odd, hot Hong Kong night.
I'm not allowed to forget:
I have no money and I'm old.

Maybe

Maybe when three sparrows
line up neatly on a swing in Yuen Long,
whoever looks on patiently enough
will win the Mark Six.

Maybe goldfish bought in Mong Kok
are telepathic and share the secrets
of their new owners. 'She is lonely.'
'This one is lonely too.'
'Nobody in the family talks.'

Maybe in the small hours
the letters on Lan Kwai Fong street signs
rearrange themselves to thwart
drunk English professors.

Maybe the stray dogs in Tin Shui Wai
are soldiers who died heroically
in the Battle of Hong Kong
reincarnated.

Maybe in the many nearby ghost towns,
ghosts do roam
and send old-fashioned good wishes
to abstract relatives in distant homes.

NOTE: Read the Word "Note" Aloud

Note: This is not the actual cover of the book
They removed the offensive artwork
and the title, which appropriates a slogan
currently deemed obsolete. *Note: Some pages
are reluctantly left blank* The writers and artists
and lawyers and professors who contributed
the material were no longer in a position
to grant us permission, either by choice
or due to death. *Note: On account
of the authenticity of "the event" being challenged,
the same said event was redacted* This erasure
applies also to poetic names of streets
which must now be metaphorical, anonymous:
miles through the snubbed streets, chaotic
classified scenes unfold in streets
that are themselves arteries threatened
to be folded up, goods and gods thrown
onto the streets, grievances on the streets
continuing into and beyond October.
*Note: There is a Cantonese note of Cantonese
contempt in some Cantonese witnesses'
Cantonese verdicts* A valid proof
that the language is versatile, versifiable
and not an error in printing. *Note: No pages
should be on display or reproduced*
The aforementioned event is a historical
placeholder, a splendid anomaly, defined
by a bold tone of definite pitch
made once by the people's voice.

14 October 2022

Teapot, Broth, Body

My city is a famed teapot.
Inside, it's darkly stained –
the colours and flavours of past
sovereigns and leaves. Every
new brew already decades old,
telling of disappointed prophecies.

My city is a boiling broth –
an everlasting stew of local bones,
foreign teeth, and ancient poison.
It's been years, this gruesome
business grinding freedoms into
fresh, urgent phantoms.

My city is a body with several tongues,
too clumsy to all fit in a stunned,
shut mouth. Words that emerge,
come out in fits and terror. Its heart
has no suburbs; all year round
it's a burning, rioting season.

19 October 2022

Removed and Rectified

you read from a distant life
it's almost back to normal
calligraphy meets glass tubes

meets flames meets memories
bright above the heads
of those who know customs

and those who stray for a while
like a garage dog or a shop cat
all things advertised: bridal

medicinal, gambling, pawning
lust in multifaceted incarnations
life is almost back to normal

on strict government orders
neon signs, glamorous, decadent
continue to come down

local trade and visual history
backdrop to at once futuristic
and nostalgic filmic wastelands

loudest and most towering
that once stood out now hang
on museum walls or reproduced

in miniatures in living rooms
from a distance your regular bus
going under the signs

you remember now takes others
to their own lopsided homes
no gatherings allowed

on strict government orders
to divert its route
regular people's feet

can't make more hopeful manifestos
for a while you read from a distance
life is almost back to normal

21 October 2022

Are You Becoming Critically Endangered?

Do you collect shiny objects? When alarmed
what plea do you make? Why do people
in your city have a penchant for joking?
What is a group of you called, as in:
a siege of cranes or a lamentation of swans?

Can you be shot legally? When was the last
time you congregated in large numbers
to unlearn self-censorship? Which factor
is the most important in determining
your carbon footprint?

Do you deploy infrasonic rumbling
to communicate with others? Are you
as a people a symbol of anything
universal? What prominent mythologies
are associated with your city?

Can you put two systems together?
Is it true that collectively you have great
long-term memory but sometimes
you opt for feigning amnesia
out of insecurity about security?

How do you vote within your packs?
In times of contention, which groups of you
have a remarkable ability to convert
themselves into warriors, revealing
tough scales, beaks, horns, or words?

Whose antlers are used to make handles
of umbrellas? If you roar to mark or defend
your territory, how far can your roar
be heard from? What help is available
for someone suffering from a phobia?

Are you social animals, like penguins,
living in colonies? How long does it take
to empty your city of its essence and ethos?
What percentage of democracy
have you explored and mapped to date?

If you were to give your mouth a name –
such as Aristotle's lantern – what would
that be? Approximately how many years
does it take to rebuild demolished piers?
Who are your power-driven predators?

How many broods of young
can your government imprison? Is your city
now one of the largest global producers
of migrants? How many heart and time
zones must your city contain?

22 October 2022

Pearls of Wisdom

How do you know a watermelon
is ready? You slap it and hear
its echoing sound.

Whoever comes to this city,
helps forge it into its current being,
can claim it and have their say.

How quickly one forgets
he who was apologetic deserves
no love from you.

An old newspaper tells
new stories every
other decade.

Tyrants will not all die.
But a people, sometimes,
may actually pay attention.

Art

For some, the art of leaving isn't hard
to master. The one-way plane tickets, the house,
possibly a backyard. The city loses something

each day: freedoms; its finest lawyers, writers,
scholars who will one day look back
at this broken ship of a town

with loving nostalgia. The art of staying, however,
must be mastered regardless of how, for those
whose roots evidently know this is the land

where their bones shall be ground to dust. The
mountains have seen their ancestors. They own
this city, this realm, even the bittersweet summer

sun. Some wonder if the harbour will smell
the same. The trees? How long will it take
before mail is confiscated? When will coins

and banknotes erase Hong Kong? Will we
speak a different tongue and become
a placid province? Going, going, gone.

after Elizabeth Bishop

At This Moment, Everyone Is a Revolution

i. Some People

Some people shed their petty personalities like snake skin, only to grow a new layer that is a strengthened version of the old. On the other side of the river, it is no longer the same river – some people accept this as fact, others secretly question it because they don't understand. One week always flows into the next and a chorus of international cameras can't reverse time, can't change some people's minds. Some people take turns to bleed for what they think is worthwhile. There are those who succumb to flattery, delighted at being called intelligent, having a good poetry ear and perfectly timed. There are those however who loathe praise, every hyperbolic word is perceived as a carefully constructed insult. In a neat room no one is foolish enough to throw the first piece of trash on the floor. In an already tarnished room, some people readily fantasize smashing its glasses and concealed windows. When some people find out they are in a novel, they demand to be given the ability to create tears, to genuinely cry. Some people sell lies. Some fabricate them as though in a party line. Some live in lies like living in a sealed showroom. Some people look on. Some take action.

13 June 2019

ii. The Fall

A note of demands on behalf of the whole city that has been battered, tortured, frustrated by the inhumane and tone-deaf government of Hong Kong: "No Extradition to China. Make Love No Shoot. Total withdrawal of the extradition bill. We are not rioters. Release the students and injured. Carrie Lam step down. Help Hong Kong." What must have gone through his mind as he fell? That he was there, and then he was no more. What does it say about a city that drives one of its own literally off a building, in public sight? We have tried and tried to make our voices heard. Some sing hymns. Some forgo food. Some make signs. Some cry in silence, trembling, nursing a lingering heartache. Do we all have to imprint notes across the city, on its mountains and

bridges and lampposts and shop fronts and park benches and walls, for
us to be finally heard? The bell tolls for us all.

15 June 2019

iii. We Are What We are Made of

Beginning from every day
tears are shed: their tails are puffs
of smoke. Beginning from yesterday
walls are covered in squared colours,
street names changed. Beginning from then
poetry can mean, be, and stay. Beginning
from June 2019, people
in a city look at each other:
million faces, million thoughts,
united in water, practice, slogans.
Beginning from now,
there is no turning back, no stopping.
We are what we are made of:
desperation and unbeatable will.
This is the beginning of the open
secret that we don't ever quit.

25 July 2019

iv. The City I Live in

On weekends, people walk the streets in the fierce sun
on the brink of fainting –
grey sweat comes down to their ankles
when a river of heads chants add oil.
At least one in seven people choose to boldly speak
a forbidden language of signs, posters, and videos;
of hope, metaphors, malls, and proliferating
Lennon Walls. The city I live in is no longer
only office buildings with glass fronts

or identical shops that sell identical
things. It is a city of diverse limbs
that each know their direction –
wherever they are needed, they go.

27 July 2019

v. This Moment

At this moment an airplane is landing. The pilot
makes the usual announcement
before explaining to passengers about the peaceful
protesters at the airport dressed in black.
He switches from English to Cantonese
to say the most heartfelt words.

At this moment a family is going to Disneyland.
A little boy is oblivious to teargas and rubber pallets,
thinking only of Mickey Mouse and Winnie the Pooh.
May he grow up to never know
the fear of being caned.
At this moment

train stations are transformed into battlegrounds,
blood of citizens on floor
like abstract calligraphy. The trains
take no one to nowhere until someone
makes some right decisions.

This moment a people is angry. They carry
on with their lives barely. How many more
days to endure for a government to listen
and show remorse?

At this moment, everyone is a revolution.

28 July 2019

vi. Anecdotes for The Future

o.
Sometimes a typhoon
is not just a natural phenomenon.
It coincides
with a movement.

o.
They would claim
they are not tyrants,
only realists, patriots.

o.
Dark night. Fireworks horizontally
deployed from a moving black car,
weapons with ringing sounds
and colours. Smoke
gets in the eyes of protesters
in the town where I grew up.

o.
A gun's mouth can point
Middle fingers of the police
are raised
All that is steel or sturdy
can become youngsters'
makeshift shields
Our full bodies are alert

o.
Near dawn, strangers
in their separate rooms, on different
sofas or looking out of their myriad
windows, collectively sigh or cry.

0.
The disobedient citizens
are determined to be,
to be disobedient,
in all parts of the city – flowers
blossom everywhere. All
walks of lives, all hues of hair,
cut open our regular existence
to forge a new Hong Kong.

31 July 2019

If I Do Not Reply

If I do not respond, think:
it must be because of the mountains.
The signal is poor here,
and all my portraits are gone

except those of me
looking angry, lost, and young.
A face from decades ago,
ancient, with no irregular lines

impressed on my forehead.
I miss my collection of random
books like an illiterate person
misses his education.

If I do not call, it's because
my blood has darkened
from I don't know what. If
I pray it's not to a god

but to the sun that brightens
generations before it dies, burnt
through the eras, the changing
codes and modes of morality.

If I do not reply, think:
it's because I have given myself
to the man-made weather.
The sea as a thick closet,

the sky is a blue ceiling, even
the trees welcome me as a rotting
singing bird. If I do not say
anything, believe me,

it's not what they tell you.
I have disappeared into a body
of mirrors, only reflecting
other mirrors, of this life.

6 February 2021

Time and Tide

時間保留

我們何時最終明白時間？
我們真的現在了解時間嗎？
星體，季節。十六世紀
無人理會

時間準確與否。無事甚急。
萬事俱略。現在，
每分每秒
能關鍵迫在眉睫的生存邊緣

與死亡，但是我們的鐘
不響不滴答，
都是電子的展示。我們要
往從前看才能向前看：

放射性碳定年告知
地球年歲： 人類歷史骨內存。
聽說將有一個新時鐘
計量文明。一滴答

已一年。我們這代亡了它還在。
希望地球能抵敵重重毀損
而時間繼續給與。
我們可以成為優良祖先嗎？

Time Keep

translated from the Chinese by the poet

When will we finally understand time?
Do we really now understand time?
Solar bodies, seasons. In the 16th century
no one cared about

the accuracy of time. Nothing was urgent.
Everything approximate. Now,
every minute and every second
can mean the imminent verge of life

and death, and yet our clocks now
don't even tick, when we look
at their digital silent displays. We need
to look back to look forward:

Radiocarbon clocks determining the age
of the earth – human histories stored in bone.
I heard a new clock is being created
to measure civilizations. It ticks just once

a year. It will outlast us all.
I hope Earth can weather the damage being done
and time keep giving.
Can we be good ancestors?

The Chinese original was broadcast as part of the "Earthsong: Science-inspired Poetry Against Climate Change" event that took place at the United Nations Climate Change Conference in Glasgow (#COP26) on Monday 1 November 2021.

Absence

I miss you
like a watch misses
being strapped to an antique

wrist; like a pair
of reading glasses
with round wooden frames

misses printed words
in a collection of prose poetry
by an old Asian American

writer who knows
not everything must be
about racing and race;

like a wall in Hong Kong
misses graffiti
screaming decay and democracy,

now covered up
by heavy strokes of grey
impermanent paint; like

a snowed-in road
misses the early signs of spring
so its tarmac surface can be seen

in its grandiose ugly urban glory;
like a luminous and poetic window
shut for too long misses

a hand to push it open to prove
it has always, always,
had it in it to let

in more light, more air;
and like a vacuum cleaner
misses dust everywhere,

which is what we are,
to which we will one day return,
to be dusted off the Earth.

7 February 2021

Keys

He's playing music again, my neighbour,
at the piano for his companions. One o'clock
in the morning. I imagine a party of five: two men,
three women. They are just hanging out
until one of them says to another: let's kiss.

My neighbour, the saxophonist
who plays the piano and who might teach me
French, is playing Erik Satie. By coincidence,
my professor likes his music, and there's a street
nearby named after the composer.

One o'clock in the morning a musician
plays the piano while his friends sit listening,
and his neighbour, me, pictures a kiss
that may or may not happen
between the keys, behind the doors.

20 November 2022

Time and Tide

Our faces glow in front of a row
of lit globes. In the shopping mall,

where we stand –
other lovers we have replaced

had also stood, counting cities
they knew

condensed into dots,
transient in their borders.

Waves somewhere keep up
an unfathomable dance,

stars revise schedules, every summer
lengthens, becoming an elegy.

Maps and globes are oblivious
to an ephemeral celestial event

that we will or will not witness.
So much depends on what is fleeting,

what isn't known, and how eager
the world turns on us by forgetting.

16 August 2019

Sometimes a Dream

In a dream my body
is large. Tables stacking up on me,
people feast while I watch.
My eyes sprout fingers.
In another dream you enter
my dream, me. You say we are
both dreamt up by another you
somewhere else eating a walnut.
A third dream hosts
only defaced books.
Some characters remain:
door, mouth, vagina, opening.
Sometimes a dream forgets
it is a dream. It unfolds a scroll
of ancient calligraphy.
Millions of people, water flows.

2019

Palm Trees

I've never touched any palm trees. I've never
touched you. I'll ask somebody to plant one
just for me. It will grow erratically but thank
goodness, trust me, my patience's

infinite. I'll sashay to it when I'm ready.
You tell me to finger its bark; it's your body
waking up from summer gales. Then I'll sit
in its spasmodic shade and contemplate

why berries consummate bruises overnight;
why small fish let themselves get caught
in sparse nets to send messages; why
roots are haunted by secondhand love

and lost deer ashes. Leaning my back
on the trunk, I'll become its auxiliary bud.
I'll think of touching you. Mostly, I'll dream
of the geometry of entwined limbs.

July and November 2012, and 17 October 2022

Inscribed

How can my messages reach you?
Pity the old courtiers who knew
only the makeup fashions
of their youth. Long enough
you've abandoned our relay stations
that bridge roads and oceans.
Another November moon's reflection,

grieving in the inquisitive river, ripples
into a cave of no circumference.
What kind of Chinese do you plough?
'Two people together is a work',
every word delicate but gutting, every word
now. Water imitates other water. Don't
let your writing brush go unused.

1 November 2022

Shared Knowledge

Love is not love if it's conditional.
Bullshit, only love that is conditional is love,
filtered through expressions of future.

Torn out of books and bookmarks, your ears
listen only to groans your body engenders
and when I moan a little out of tune,

you wonder how made-believe love
can sustain us. How our shared knowledge
of the cosmos makes us

a better couple of whiny lovers
knowing too well it's not at all simple
to love. It's not easy, at all,

to admit failure. But we come,
only seconds apart. And
our bookshelves align,

our faces face the same direction.
We reflect naked in the mirrors,
deeply, deeply, deeply, in love.

Your Palms

I like your palms large enough
for me to practise
writing complicated
traditional Chinese characters –
every one is an enigma, every one
a prediction. Our hip and shoulder bones
are barely covered by our flesh and skin
when afternoon lights are capricious
and unknowing. We have been eaten up
by this city's grief and desire. Tonight
a poet told me 69 is the number of poems
in his book, and a community
is connected with the rest of the world.
Another said a dove, an umbrella
and a discoloured bauhinia, together,
create the story of Hong Kong. A professor
postulated that there are only three topics
worth researching in the universe.
From one celestial star
to the next, from you to your love – me,
a dress may rekindle translated memories,
a glare may start a history. I mistook
a canal lock as a love lock. But I remember
your fingers, whirling, trying to write,
and much more.

He Promised Me He'll Speak
Only Cantonese on Fridays

A promise I didn't reciprocate.
I also didn't promise him:
My hair will stop falling on the bed,
Past, present and future co-exist,
All language disputes be settled,
Democracies have no famines.
I didn't promise him:
Poems tossed into sleepless nights,
Mirrors reflect us weekly,
Umbrellas can only be opened,
Kowloon and Hong Kong Island meet.
Instead, I promised him:
It matters that our tongues agree,
Body landscapes will be remembered,
Everything around us is already present,
We'll write, be hungry, and very quoted.

Translated

The next world, if there is one, may not be free of boredom.
You prefer to be a door than a wall, open
to new interpretations, defying what people think
homonyms can do. We are collectors of moments –
cataloguing them, giving them novel names.
Do I inspire rebellion or obedience?
Once things are damaged, we fix them,
but are they still the same? So many art terms I should know,
and nothing is untranslatable, you insist.
You are always risking morality and fidelity.
If you demolish me, you promise to relocate me
in your notebook, in another language.
You said you need stress in your life, then I show up.
Your face has many symbols of prejudices.
Some people are textually repressed, you taught me.
What makes a beard attractive?
What makes an old notice board noticeable?
For you, every word is another word, and surprises are tender.
You have begun to write poems
that speak of cats and bamboo scaffolding
and Kowloon and time travel. Are there
things that, in your absence, can be used
to reconstruct you? You remain relevant,
making love in several languages.
You have worn grammar to deflect insecurity.
Many singular events form a translation. Your fingers
are a source of power, for
assertive translations are arousing.
How many people can own the rights to your work
at the same time? How many your heart?
You said I boost your memory
when I hold grudges and repeat accusations.
Texts recreated by you are famous.
The joy and pain of knowing that words matter.
You forbid me to speak to any other translator.

Your Name in My Lexicon Means Yes

Once, you talked to me on the phone,
I complained about the loud wind
obscuring your voice. You responded:
Baby, I can't make the wind stop.

Navigation

To go from here to there, sometimes a map is needed. But some maps may lie, make up cities, towns. Some maps are only gestural, distorting the distance between separated lovers who in the old days occupied post offices with frequent letters. There is always an accurate time on a clock pinned to a wall somewhere, but not here. Censorship doesn't happen to language only, but to maps too. Entire nuclear waste dumps, detention camps, vanish. There is no standardisation of maps like the standardisation of time-zones in China. The average day is 23 hours, 56 minutes and 4.09 seconds. The average human orgasm is more fleeting than the average pig's. A rose by another name is still a rose, but there are over 900 types of red roses. A language becomes extinct every two weeks. Every time we say goodbye, think, a part of you goes extinct. There are colours that trigger hunger, others induce fear, others still make me think of your book covers. How many roads does a random map actually cover? How many days does a map know? Some countries believe printing their own maps creates a grand reality. They say in a lifetime, people brush their teeth so many times, open the venetian blinds, light a cigarette, throw out rotting flowers, pour wine – everything has an estimated number. In my lifetime, I may only see you as often as conscience lets me. There are mirrors on the moon, reflecting light. Our room has mirrors and they reflect just us, creating an epoch of our own. A new time.

Favourites

vade mecum (n.): a favourite book carried everywhere. Literally, 'go with me'. Great piece on Liu Xia – my favourite: 'As the evening cooled, she put on a tattered black sweater. A guest came over and proffered a pack of Gauloises cigarettes. Liu plucked one out. "Are these really the cigarettes French intellectuals smoke?" she asked.'

The poet says in an interview, 'My favourite poem is one that I haven't yet written.' If I told you that you were my favourite, what colour would you sing? Some of e.e. cummings's favourite words: 'young', 'sudden', 'keen', 'delicious', 'kiss', 'thrilling', 'sweet'. Xi Xi, one of my favourite writers, once said: 'You need alternatives to mainstream voices, and to give them greater parity with others.'

My favourite Christmas picture is an accidental selfie of my parents and me in front of a finished pot of Taiwanese noodles. Another favourite picture: a former student sat next to me on the bus from the TVB studio to the nearest MTR station. *BoJack Horseman* is one of my favourite shows. BoJack: 'I felt like a xerox of a xerox of a person.' *The Prestige* is still my most favourite Christopher Nolan film. A few years ago, 2,000 people were polled – favourite positions for men: doggie, cowgirl and missionary. For women: doggie, missionary and cowgirl.

The London-based poet Ian McLachlan said, 'My favourite pick-up line is found in Francis Ford Coppola's *Dracula*. Dracula to Mina: "Do not fear me!" A winner every time. Every time.' This is one of my all-time favourite Hong Kong dishes: Rice with ham, spam and a fried egg. Lots of sweet cooked soy sauce. One of my favourite observations of art, made by Zadie Smith, in relation to Balthasar Denner's painting *Alte Frau*: '[W]hat men consider enigmatic in women is actually agency.' The *South China Morning Post* featured my most favourite professor, Douglas Kerr. The Italian photographer Gabriele Galimberti took pictures of kids from around the globe alongside their favourite toys.

One of my favourite writers, John Berger, believed that the act of lovemaking can temporarily accommodate the complete feeling of being in love and that being desired may allow one to reach a sense of immortality. One of my favourite episodes of *Black Mirror* is San Junipero; my heart aches for any kind of love that is misplaced, that cannot be. Another favourite writer, Umberto Eco: 'Any fact becomes important when it's connected to another.' One of my favourite directors, Jia Zhangke: 'There are a lot of colloquialisms in the Cantonese language that can never be represented aptly in Mandarin.'

Dung Kai-cheung: 'My favourite film director is Andrei Tarkovsky. In *Vivi and Vera*, there are a whole host of images and some very quiet scenes, where time seems to stop. Tarkovsky could have been at the back of my mind when I wrote them.' Once, Virginia Woolf snappily responded to the remark 'a deceased man of letters whose character you most dislike.' Woolf: 'I like all dead men of letters.' One of my favourite films, *Rouge*, stars Leslie Cheung and Anita Mui. Promises vanish like words written in smoke.

This is a story by Lydia Davis. Reading it saddens me – A writer who doesn't have a favourite story that she herself has written. A man who doesn't have a happiest moment that he himself has experienced. Borrowed story. Borrowed moment.

Pillow Books

[1] *Things that quicken the heart/give you goose bumps* – A Saturday morning latte, sprinkled with nutmeg. A cup of warm red wine infused with cinnamon. The wails of the neighbour's cat – more human than feline. The alarm at 2.00 a.m. The thud of a book landing at the stoop. The lights coming down at the theatre. The opening chords of 'Helplessness Blues'.

[2] *Things that rise* – Banana bread. The sun, every morning, even though I may not see much of it. Boiling water. Friends' pregnant tummies. A dozing cat roused by a distinctive sound. Nipples aroused by a distinctive touch.

[3] *A thing that surprised me at first* – Being called "luv" by a complete stranger.

[4] *Mysterious things* – How one supermarket can close at five, when its neighbour closes at nine. The difference between brands of washing powder. What a partner sees when he goes running alone. A photograph of my family which cannot be deleted from a memory card and follows me from camera to camera.

[5] *At seven o'clock last night,* my partner returned from work. He stood outside the door, adjusted his red scarf and then walked away to get the milk he always forgets. Ten minutes later, he reappeared with a Tesco bag, claiming he had come straight from the train and had only now just arrived. I was highly suspicious, especially since he smelled faintly of beer. It did not occur to me until later that there is no Tesco nearby.

[6] *Memories of my grandfather* – Peanut-buttered bread. Empty peanut-butter jars, scraped nearly clean, lined up on the far end of the table. His wooden staff. Him, sitting alone on a bench in the playground. His smile when he saw my sisters and I skipping rope.

[7] *Infuriating things* – A person you are fond of turns out to be far less worthy than you thought. Discovering that an image you thought

original has been used before. Delayed trains. Departing trains that squeak too loud. Someone's underwear – visible beneath his loose jeans. A still-lit cigarette thrown in a bush. When you are wearing your tallest heels and the elevators in the Russell Square station aren't working so you have to climb the 117 steps. When receiving guests in your house, you see a cobweb that you had not noticed before. Fine hair above the lip. Shadows that bear little resemblance to their owners. A recalled library book. A paper clip that doesn't clip. A zigzag in a pair of stockings that leads everybody to speculate on its cause. An inadequate supply of chilli oil at dim sum. After you spill wine on your keyboard, and the keys stick and produce random letters.

[8] *The electronics graveyard in the closet* – Three digital cameras. Every generation of iPod. Headphones. Discordant cords. Keyless keyboards. Wireless mice. Once loved brands, now out of favour.

[9] *One day a Jehovah's Witness came to the door* and promised to return with a Chinese Bible. The next day he delivered the book as promised, and he asked when he should come again. When I told him "in one year," the disappointment on his face almost made me convert.

[10] *Things that someone else takes care of* – Hair mice in the shower drain. Contact lens cases. Leftover soup in a Nissin cup noodle. The cup itself. Orange peels. Fallen leaves that sneak past the door. A dead spider.

[11] *Kinds of days* – Dewy days. Due days. Productive days. Reproductive days. Redo days.

[12] *Things that sadden the heart* – That each lover is not a recapitulation of all those loved before and after. A white cloth that is no longer white. A hole visible when the nail is pulled out. The removed second place setting at a table for one.

[13] *Things that give me pleasure* – It is pleasing to unexpectedly discover a particular Cantonese dish you love on the menu of a local restaurant. Seeing herons along a bridge. Deleting junk emails *en masse*. Returning

a dropped coin to its owner. Brushing my teeth for five minutes, undisturbed. Seeing my mom comb her thick hair like a young girl. Feeling the stubble on the sweetheart's face. When the pot of morning coffee turns out perfect, not too bitter or too watery. That every day is not like the next. That as John Steinbeck said, "Nothing good gets away." When my name is uttered softly or raindrops on the windowpane doodle a letter. Well-worn boots. The smell of new books. The smell of old books. Being praised, even stutteringly. Being admonished by someone I love and who means well. Being reminded of something in a timely manner. Listening to my father sing old Mandarin songs, perfectly-pitched and confident – something which has not happened for three years.

[14] *Things to have when sleeping* – The light on. Two bottles of water. A stifling number of blankets. Six pillows to my partner's one, including two orthopaedic. Soft-covered books which can double as pillows in an emergency.

Salpetrière

My heart, away from the pulse of a peeling
home, has gone on strike.

It has at least slowed down –
Have there been any sudden deaths

in the family? I breathe through
a large white tank like a scuba diver

back on dry land. Time is now measured
by the shadows on a bottle of hand gel.

I've never seen so much blood
in test tubes, each bearing a label

with my date of birth, a long barcode,
and my Chinese name in English.

Are you Mme Ho? How to be wheeled
down silent corridors when your desire to test

the echo of your voice is strong?
How to be a mannequin sprouting

needles and patches of swollen
skin? How to be still and balance

a perfect jar of urine – a sequel
to a painting by Magritte? In a darkened

room, the floor is flooded with blue light;
I'm an alien resting in profile. The sounds

of a heart, an adult heart, mine –
the size of two fists. There's no illusion

of another's heart. My past and present
converge, miles of translatable

beating, blooming – I'm at once
a baby and dynasties old.

Monday 3 October 2022

Milton Keynes UK
Ingram Content Group UK Ltd.
UKHW010856070424
440703UK00001B/2